The Forgotten Heist: A Race Against Time

Introduction

In the heart of a bustling metropolis, a notorious art heist occurs, but the stolen masterpiece is no ordinary painting. It holds a secret that could change the course of history once it is revealed. Known for her ability to solve the most baffling cases, Detective Erik Larsson is called in to unravel the mystery. He must decipher cryptic clues left behind by the thieves as he delves deeper into the twisted world of art, conspiracy, and betrayal. Despite facing adversaries who will stop at nothing to protect the secret, Erik races against time to recover the stolen artwork and uncover the truth.

For readers who enjoy solving puzzles and unraveling enigmatic plots, this mystery and thriller eBook combines art, history, and suspense.

Content

PROLOGUE: THE STOLEN MASTERPIECE

The city of Stockholm was dark and quiet. The only sounds were the occasional car and the flicker of streetlights. Inside the Stockholm Museum of Art, a priceless painting called "The Enigma of Eternity" hung in the dimly lit gallery. It was the centerpiece of the museum's collection and had captivated art enthusiasts from around the world.

Unbeknownst to anyone, a group of audacious criminals had been planning a heist of epic proportions. They descended upon the museum dressed in all-black attire, moving with precision and purpose. The leader of the group, known as "The Maestro," had orchestrated successful heists before and intended to make "The Enigma of Eternity" his crowning achievement.

The painting was protected by an unbeatable security system of security lasers connected to alarms. The Maestro and his team had a plan to disable the lasers temporarily and make their escape before the system was reactivated. They used smoke machines and cutting-edge technology to manipulate the lasers, creating a temporary corridor of safety through which they could pass.

"The Enigma of Eternity" was gently lifted from its place on the wall, causing a gasp of disbelief to echo through the room. The painting held a secret that, once unveiled, could change the course of history. With the masterpiece in hand, the criminals slipped away into the night, leaving no trace of their presence except for the empty frame hanging in the gallery.

The museum's alarms sounded, and security personnel rushed to the scene, but they were too late. The city of Stockholm and the art world would soon learn of the audacious heist, but the true significance of "The Enigma of Eternity" and the mystery it held were known only to The Maestro and his team.

Detective Erik Larsson received a mysterious phone call that would forever change the course of his life. And so, the stage was set for an unforgettable journey of intrigue, suspense, and a relentless pursuit of the truth.

CHAPTER 1:

THE CALL TO DUTY

DETECTIVE ERIK LARSSON'S REPUTATION

Erik Larsson was a seasoned investigator in Stockholm's police force, who had earned a reputation for his unrelenting dedication to solving complex cases that left others baffled. He was well-known for his sharp mind, remarkable intuition, and unwavering commitment which made him stand out in the world of law enforcement.

Larsson's journey into the realm of crime-solving had been challenging. He grew up in a neighbourhood plagued by crime in the heart of Stockholm. Nevertheless, these early experiences instilled in him a fierce determination to bring justice to the streets he had once called home.

His relentless pursuit of the truth had led him to solve several high-profile cases, earning him the admiration of his peers and the respect of his superiors. The media often referred to him as "The Detective with the Unbreakable Resolve."

However, Erik Larsson had his own demons, and behind his stoic exterior was a man haunted by the memories of a tragedy that had struck his family years ago. It was a personal loss that ignited his passion for justice and fuelled his unwavering commitment to his work.

THE MYSTERIOUS PHONE CALL THAT CHANGES EVERYTHING

It was a cold and rainy evening, and Larsson was getting ready to leave the police station. Suddenly, his phone rang, breaking the silence of his office. He answered, anticipating a routine call or maybe a colleague seeking advice. However, the voice on the other end was not what he expected. It was a voice he hadn't heard in years, a voice he wished never to hear again.

The voice sent shivers down his spine as it was from his past, which he had buried long ago. It was an old friend, a contact from a part of his life he thought was over. The friend spoke in cryptic terms, implying about a heist at the Stockholm Museum of Art. The masterpiece stolen was called "The Enigma of Eternity," and it held a secret of immense importance that only Larsson could unravel.

As the voice continued speaking, Larsson was torn between the haunting memories of his past and his responsibility as a detective. The call set in motion a chain of events that would lead him into a world of intrigue, art, and a relentless pursuit of the truth.

Erik Larsson realized he was being called to duty once again, to solve a mystery that would not only test his detective skills but also force him to confront the demons of his past. The heist at the museum was just the beginning of a journey that would change his life forever.

CHAPTER 2:

THE CRYPTIC CLUES

UNRAVELING THE MESSAGE LEFT BEHIND

Erik Larsson didn't waste any time. He immediately gathered a small team of trusted investigators and hurried to the Stockholm Museum of Art, where the heist had taken place. The empty frame on the wall of the gallery where "The Enigma of Eternity" had once hung was a stark reminder of the audacity of the thieves.

The crime scene was complex and intriguing. The smoke residue from the thieves' clever diversion was still in the air, and the security lasers had been expertly manipulated to allow the criminals access to the painting. But the most fascinating aspect of the scene was the series of mysterious symbols and riddles left behind by the thieves.

Larsson examined the symbols carefully, which were engraved into the marble floor and the cryptic messages that were written on the walls. They were beautifully crafted and hinted at the intelligence of the thieves. It was clear that they wanted to leave their mark, taunt and challenge those who pursued them.

Larsson's team worked tirelessly to document and decode the symbols. They worked deep into the night to figure out the messages. Clues began to emerge as they pieced together the elements of the puzzle. The symbols led to a series of numbers and letters, hinting at a hidden message that held the key to the stolen painting's true meaning.

THE RACE TO DECIPHER THE CODE

As time passed, Larsson realized that the painting theft was not just a simple crime. It left a trail of clues that seemed to indicate that "The Enigma of Eternity" painting was not just an artwork, but also held a secret that had been kept hidden for generations.

Larsson and his team worked tirelessly to decode the message, which led them to historical references, ancient manuscripts, and hidden symbols in the painting itself. Every second was crucial, as the thieves were getting further away.

The investigation was like a puzzle, with each piece revealing a part of the truth. As Larsson continued, he realized that "The Enigma of Eternity" held the key to a secret that had been buried for centuries, a secret that could change history.

The race to decipher the code had begun, and Erik Larsson knew he was not only competing against the criminals, but also against time. The answers were hidden in the cryptic clues left by the thieves, waiting to be uncovered.

CHAPTER 3:

THE WORLD OF ART AND DECEPTION

EXPLORING THE ART WORLD'S SECRETS

Erik Larsson's investigation uncovered a layer of intrigue surrounding "The Enigma of Eternity" that went beyond its role as a stolen masterpiece. As he delved deeper into the world of art and deception, he realized that the painting was not a unique case but part of a much larger puzzle.

Larsson immersed himself in the labyrinthine world of art, attending gallery openings, conversing with eccentric collectors, and rubbing shoulders with renowned artists. The more he delved into this elite circle, the more he came to understand the hidden complexities of the art world. It was a realm where beauty concealed secrets, where priceless masterpieces held untold stories, and where every brushstroke could be a clue to an enigma.

He discovered that "The Enigma of Eternity" was part of a series of paintings, each connected by a common theme and a shared secret. The stolen painting was not the only work of art with a hidden message. He began to examine the other works in the series, searching for clues that could illuminate the true significance of the stolen masterpiece.

SUSPECTS AND MOTIVES

As Larsson delved deeper into the secrets of the art world, he discovered a list of suspects, each with a motive that complicated the investigation. The reason for the theft was unclear, but it was evident that "The Enigma of Eternity" was more crucial than just its artistic value.

The suspects included influential art collectors, each with their own obsessions and ambitions. Viktor Nordström, a reclusive billionaire known for his vast art collection and penchant for secrecy, was one of them. Isabella Forsberg, an enigmatic art dealer with a reputation for brokering deals in the shadows, was another. Lars and Helena Bergman, a wealthy couple with a deep connection to the art world and their own secrets, were the final suspects.

The motives of these individuals were as intricate as the paintings they desired. Some were after power and prestige, while others were driven by an unquenchable thirst for knowledge and hidden truths. Larsson's mission was to unravel the web of relationships, rivalries, and secrets that had ensnared the art world.

As he interrogated each suspect and explored the enigmatic world of art, Larsson's investigation deepened, causing him to question not only the stolen masterpiece but also the very essence of art itself. The lines between beauty and deception, creation and destruction, were blurred, and he realized that the key to solving the mystery lay at the intersection of these worlds, waiting to be discovered.

CHAPTER 4:

THE HEIST'S ENIGMATIC LEADER

A MASTERMIND BEHIND THE CRIME

As Erik Larsson and his team continued their investigation, it became increasingly evident that the daring heist at the Stockholm Museum of Art was carried out by a mastermind criminal, known as "The Maestro," who had successfully evaded law enforcement agencies around the world. This notorious leader had a fearsome reputation that struck fear into the hearts of both detectives and collectors.

The Maestro was a mysterious figure, who had concealed his true identity behind layers of fake names and trails. He was believed to be an expert in disguise, having the uncanny ability to blend in with any environment. His intelligence and cunning were legendary, and his crimes were marked by an exceptional level of planning and attention to detail.

Larsson delved into The Maestro's history of high-stakes heists, which spanned across continents. Each of his crimes had left a trail of destruction and intrigue, with the stolen artifacts often holding secrets and enigmas of their own. The Maestro's motives remained unknown, and his true purpose was only known to himself.

Larsson's pursuit to uncover The Maestro's identity took him through numerous encounters with international law enforcement agencies, all of whom had been baffled by the criminal's elusive nature. Interpol's files contained little information on the Maestro, who appeared to leave no trace, fingerprints, or witnesses.

THE CHASE BEGINS

Determined to bring The Maestro to justice, Larsson launched a global manhunt. He collaborated with detectives from around the world who had encountered the criminal's handiwork. The pursuit spanned across borders and through a web of international connections.

Despite each step in the investigation, The Maestro managed to stay one step ahead. The clues and leads led to dead ends, and the detective found himself in a relentless game of cat and mouse. It was a chase that would test his skills, intellect, and resilience like never before.

As Larsson delved deeper into The Maestro's world, he realized that this was not merely a pursuit of a criminal but a battle of wits and determination. The stolen masterpiece, "The Enigma of Eternity," was not just a work of art. It was a pawn in a game that had been set in motion long before the heist.

The chase had begun. As Larsson delved deeper into the shadows, he knew that the enigmatic leader was watching, waiting, and orchestrating the next move. The race to capture The Maestro had only just begun, and it was a race that would push Larsson to his limits and force him to confront the mysteries of the criminal mind.

CHAPTER 5:

THE ART OF DECEPTION

LIES AND TRUTHS INTERTWINED

As Detective Erik Larsson delved deeper into the world of art and deception, he began to realize that it was becoming increasingly difficult to differentiate between reality and illusion. The investigation into the stolen masterpiece titled "The Enigma of Eternity" had taken him into a realm where truth and lies were so intricately intertwined that it was almost impossible to distinguish one from the other.

In his quest for the truth, Larsson came across a network of art forgers and counterfeiters. It soon became apparent that the stolen painting was not the only masterpiece with a secret. The art world was rife with forgeries and replicas, each crafted with such precision that they could easily deceive collectors and art enthusiasts.

Larsson had to navigate through a maze of deceit as he examined paintings that bore the hallmarks of deception. The forgers had become experts at replicating the styles of famous artists, making it increasingly difficult to distinguish between authentic and counterfeit works. In this world of illusion, the detective had to rely on his intuition and sharp eye to uncover the truth.

The investigation led him to the shady underbelly of the art market, where deals were made in secret and reputations were built on falsehoods. As Larsson questioned artists, collectors, and dealers, he soon realized that the art of deception was not limited to just the counterfeit works, but it extended to the very people who inhabited this enigmatic world.

A TRAIL OF FORGED MASTERPIECES

Larsson was determined to uncover the truth, leading him to follow a trail of counterfeit masterpieces, each of which contained a piece of the puzzle. The forgers had left behind hidden symbols and codes within their replicas, implying a connection to "The Enigma of Eternity" and the theft carried out by The Maestro.

The detective's team meticulously examined each counterfeit painting, searching for the secrets concealed within. The path of deception led them to a group of skilled artisans who had been enticed into the world of forgery with promises of wealth and anonymity. These artisans were both victims and conspirators in a grand scheme of art deceit.

As Larsson continued to peel away the layers of lies and truths, he realized that the stolen masterpiece was not merely a work of art but a key to unlocking a hidden world of secrets and conspiracies. The forgeries held the clues to a larger puzzle, one that extended far beyond the stolen painting itself.

With each discovery, the detective moved closer to uncovering the true significance of "The Enigma of Eternity" and its connection to The Maestro. The art of deception had become a central theme in the investigation, and Larsson realized that it was a theme that would shape the course of the mystery, revealing a world where truth and illusion coexisted in a delicate balance.

CHAPTER 6:

THE GALLERY OF BETRAYAL

UNMASKING TRAITORS WITHIN THE ART COMMUNITY

Erik Larsson was investigating the theft of the masterpiece "The Enigma of Eternity" when he discovered a web of betrayal within the art community. As he dug deeper, he realized that deception and treachery were rampant at every level of the art world. Some famous artists had created counterfeit pieces, selling them as originals and betraying the trust of their admirers and collectors. Art dealers had knowingly sold forgeries, putting profit before integrity.

Larsson's investigation revealed a world where reputations were built on lies and trust was scarce. The gallery of betrayal extended beyond the stolen painting and the forgeries; it had infiltrated every corner of the art community, corrupting its very essence.

As Larsson exposed the traitors, he faced a moral dilemma. Some had been victims of their own ambition, succumbing to the allure of wealth and fame. Others had deliberately conspired to deceive and manipulate, leaving a trail of disillusioned art enthusiasts in their wake.

A WEB OF CONSPIRACY

As Larsson delved deeper into the matter, he realized that the gallery of betrayal was not just a collection of isolated incidents, but rather a part of a larger, interconnected web of conspiracy. The stolen masterpiece was the focal point of this conspiracy, and it seemed that The Maestro had orchestrated the theft to expose the dark underbelly of the art world's deceit.

The detective's investigation took him to hidden meetings, secret agreements, and shadowy alliances that operated in the shadows of the art world. The web of conspiracy was extensive, with its roots extending to unexpected places. As Larsson followed the threads of deception, he uncovered a plot that went beyond art forgery and theft.

The motives of those involved in the conspiracy varied, ranging from personal vendettas to a desire for power and control. Larsson had to determine who among them had been manipulated by The Maestro and who had willingly participated in the criminal's plan.

The gallery of betrayal and the web of conspiracy became the center of Larsson's investigation, as he sought to identify the individuals responsible for the theft and expose the extent of their treachery. It was a journey that led him further down the rabbit hole of deception, where the line between truth and deceit was constantly shifting, and where the stolen masterpiece was just one piece of a much larger puzzle.

Chapter 7:

The Clock is Ticking

The Countdown to Revelation

As the days went by, the stolen artwork called "The Enigma of Eternity" slowly revealed its secrets. It was like a mysterious clock ticking away, leading to a moment of revelation. Erik Larsson and his team had managed to decipher the hidden messages, exposed the world of art forgery, and unmasked traitors within the art community. But now, they were running out of time to uncover the ultimate truth.

The cryptic clues, forged masterpieces, and the web of conspiracy had all pointed to one thing: the stolen painting held a secret of immense historical and intellectual significance. This secret had been kept hidden for centuries, and now Larsson had to race against the clock to make sure it didn't fall into the wrong hands.

The detective knew that The Maestro, the mastermind behind the heist, was also closing in on the truth. This criminal had outsmarted law enforcement agencies across the globe, and Larsson was determined not to become another victim of The Maestro's cunning.

Racing against adversaries

Larsson was determined to uncover the truth and faced formidable enemies who were after the hidden secret for their own gain. He had to confront not only the criminal mastermind but also those who were unknowingly involved in The Maestro's web of deceit.

The detective's opponents included art collectors who believed that the stolen painting held the key to power and prestige. Some were willing to go to great lengths to obtain it, including using intimidation and blackmail. Others were obsessed with uncovering hidden truths and were driven to desperate measures.

Larsson also encountered opposition from within the art community, where loyalties and rivalries ran deep. Some members sought to protect the reputation of the art world, fearing that the painting's secret could damage its integrity. Others were manipulated by The Maestro, coerced into carrying out the criminal's plans without fully understanding the consequences.

As time was running out, Larsson had to outmaneuver his enemies and reveal the hidden secret in a way that preserved its historical and intellectual significance. The countdown to revelation had begun, and the detective's pursuit of the truth became a race against time, where every moment counted, and the ultimate revelation awaited, ready to reshape history.

CHAPTER 8:

THE UNVEILING

THE MOMENT OF TRUTH

Detective Erik Larsson's journey, which began with the daring heist at the Stockholm Museum of Art, had led him to a critical moment - the revelation of the hidden secret within "The Enigma of Eternity." As the clock ticked relentlessly, he stood on the verge of a revelation that could alter the course of history.

In a secure and undisclosed location, Larsson had assembled a group of experts, historians, and art scholars. Together, they examined the stolen masterpiece, "The Enigma of Eternity," with a mixture of excitement and trepidation. Having pieced together the cryptic clues, forged masterpieces, and uncovered the web of conspiracy, they had finally arrived at this moment.

As the painting was carefully placed under the focused beams of light, the hidden secrets within began to emerge. The art scholars and historians deciphered the intricate symbols and messages within the artwork. It became apparent that the painting was more than just a work of art; it was a vessel of knowledge, a repository of hidden truths that had been preserved for centuries.

A SHOCKING DISCOVERY

The room was filled with shockwaves of revelation. "The Enigma of Eternity" held a hidden message that uncovered a historical discovery of unparalleled significance. The painting contained a secret code that led to a long-lost manuscript, written by a renowned philosopher and scientist during the Renaissance era.

This manuscript was believed to be destroyed for centuries, but it contained groundbreaking theories and knowledge that could revolutionize the fields of science and philosophy. The discovery was a testament to the genius of the past and the power of art to preserve and convey knowledge through centuries.

The room was filled with shock and amazement as the implications of the revelation began to sink in. The stolen masterpiece, the cryptic clues, the forgeries, and the web of conspiracy had all been part of a grand plan by The Maestro to bring this hidden knowledge to light.

The revelation left Larsson and his team with a sense of awe and reverence. They had uncovered a secret that transcended art and delved into the realm of human knowledge and history. It was a discovery that would reshape the understanding of the past and open new frontiers in the world of science and philosophy.

As the world learned of the shocking discovery, "The Enigma of Eternity" ceased to be merely a stolen masterpiece; it became a symbol of the power of art to preserve and convey knowledge. The detective's journey had brought this revelation to light. The enigma had been unravelled, the secrets unveiled, and a new chapter in history had begun.

CHAPTER 9:

THE FINAL CONFRONTATION

SHOWDOWN WITH THE HEIST LEADER

The revelation of the hidden secret within "The Enigma of Eternity" had caused shockwaves not only in the world of art and academia but also in the criminal underworld. The Maestro, who was the enigmatic leader behind the audacious heist, had orchestrated the theft to bring the hidden knowledge to light. At present, he was closing in on the detective who had unravelled his grand plan.

Erik Larsson had understood The Maestro's motives and methods, but the criminal remained a shadowy figure, always one step ahead. As the detective prepared to confront the enigmatic leader, he knew that the showdown would be a battle of wits, determination, and, above all, a battle for the truth.

The Maestro had outwitted law enforcement agencies worldwide, but he had never encountered a detective as unyielding as Larsson. The final confrontation would take place in a setting that was both symbolic and dramatic—the very location where the stolen masterpiece had been unveiled to the world.

THE FATE OF THE STOLEN MASTERPIECE

Larsson and his team awaited the arrival of The Maestro, knowing that the fate of the stolen masterpiece hung in the balance. The revelation of the hidden secret within the painting had given it a new level of importance, both as a work of art and as a vessel of knowledge.

The detective had to ensure that the stolen painting was preserved and protected, remaining a symbol of the power of art to convey historical and intellectual significance. The Enigma of Eternity's fate was intrinsically tied to the outcome of the final confrontation.

The moment arrived as The Maestro, still hidden behind a mask and a veil of secrecy, entered the room. The detective and the criminal locked eyes, each recognizing the determination and resolve in the other. It was a battle of intellect, a clash of wills, and a confrontation that would determine the course of their respective destinies.

As the tension in the room mounted, Larsson and The Maestro engaged in a battle of words and revelations. The criminal defended his actions as a means to expose the hidden knowledge, while the detective questioned the ethics of his methods and the consequences of his crimes.

The stolen masterpiece became the fulcrum on which the confrontation rested. It was a symbol of the art world's resilience and its ability to preserve and convey knowledge. As the showdown reached its climax, the ultimate decision lay in whether The Maestro would allow the painting to be preserved as a symbol of discovery or attempt to reclaim it for his own purposes.

The final confrontation would determine not only the fate of the stolen masterpiece but also the fate of The Maestro and the legacy of the detective who pursued him. It was a battle of ideals and the pursuit of truth, and the outcome would leave an indelible mark on the world of art, history, and knowledge.

CHAPTER 10:

THE SECRET'S LEGACY

THE AFTERMATH OF THE HEIST'S REVELATION

The revelation of the hidden secret within "The Enigma of Eternity" caused shockwaves not only in the art world but also beyond it. Erik Larsson's tireless pursuit of the truth had finally unravelled the mysteries behind the audacious heist, exposing a web of deception and an enigmatic leader known as The Maestro. It turned out that The Maestro had orchestrated the theft to bring hidden knowledge to light.

The aftermath of the revelation was a whirlwind of media attention, academic discussions, and public fascination. The stolen masterpiece had become a symbol of the power of art to convey historical and intellectual significance. It was celebrated as a testament to the resilience of the art world.

Larsson's dedication and the work of his team had not only uncovered a hidden truth but had also exposed the corruption within the art community and the treacherous path of those who had been unwittingly ensnared in The Maestro's web of deception.

THE PAINTING'S TRUE SIGNIFICANCE

As the world came to terms with the significance of "The Enigma of Eternity," it revealed a hidden secret within the painting that led to the discovery of a long-lost manuscript. The manuscript was written by a renowned philosopher and scientist from the Renaissance era, containing groundbreaking theories and knowledge that could revolutionize the fields of science and philosophy.

The painting was now seen as a vessel of knowledge, a repository of historical and intellectual treasures. It had not only preserved a hidden truth but had also conveyed it through the ages, defying the forces of destruction and the passage of time.

The revelation sparked a renewed interest in art as a medium of knowledge and preservation. The stolen masterpiece had become a symbol of the art world's capacity to transcend aesthetics and delve into the realm of history, science, and philosophy. It was a legacy that would leave a lasting mark on the world of art and academia.

As Erik Larsson reflected on the journey that led to this moment, he realized that the pursuit of truth and the preservation of knowledge were ideals worth fighting for. The stolen masterpiece and the revelation of its hidden secret had become a testament to the resilience of the human spirit and the power of art to convey the legacy of the past.

The legacy of "The Enigma of Eternity" will continue to inspire artists, scholars, and art enthusiasts for generations to come, serving as a reminder that the secrets of the past are waiting to be uncovered, and the mysteries of history are ready to be revealed. It is a legacy that endures, transcending the confines of time and space, and ensuring that the secrets of the past are preserved for the future generations.

EPILOGUE: A NEW BEGINNING

CLOSURE AND CONSEQUENCES

The Enigma of Eternity's hidden secret was revealed, and this led to the closure of the audacious heist and the enigmatic leader known as The Maestro. Erik Larsson, the detective, fulfilled his duty by exposing the criminal's motives and methods and ensuring that the stolen masterpiece would be preserved as a symbol of the art world's resilience.

The revelation had far-reaching consequences that affected the art world and criminal underworld. Some of those ensnared in The Maestro's web of deception faced legal consequences for their actions while others sought redemption and a chance to rebuild their lives.

Larsson had demonstrated that the pursuit of truth and justice could transcend the boundaries of art and reveal the hidden secrets of history and knowledge. The detective's relentless dedication had become a source of inspiration for his peers, and his journey had left an indelible mark on the world of law enforcement.

A HINT OF NEW MYSTERIES TO COME

As the investigation drew to a close, there were hints of new mysteries on the horizon. The revelation of hidden knowledge within "The Enigma of Eternity" had sparked an insatiable curiosity for the past and the secrets it held.

Erik Larsson's journey had shown that the mysteries of history were waiting to be uncovered, and the world was filled with untold stories, hidden truths, and unexplored realms of knowledge. The detective had opened the door to a world of discovery where the pursuit of truth would continue to reveal the enigmas of the past.

The epilogue marked a new beginning, a fresh chapter in the detective's life, and a world of new mysteries waiting to be explored. The stolen masterpiece and the legacy it left behind were testament to the enduring power of art to convey the secrets of history. It was a reminder that the pursuit of truth was a journey without end.

As Erik Larsson looked to the future, he knew that the world was filled with hidden secrets waiting to be uncovered and revealed. The legacy of "The Enigma of Eternity" would continue to inspire, and the detective's journey had only just begun. It was a new beginning, a fresh start, and a hint of new mysteries to come.

ABOUT THE AUTHOR

The author of this captivating and enigmatic book **Mr. Nana Kojo Sei** is a skilled storyteller with a profound love for weaving intricate narratives that blend mystery, art, and the pursuit of truth. Known for his ability to craft engaging stories that keep readers on the edge of their seats, the author's writing style is marked by its vivid descriptions, well-defined characters, and an innate talent for creating a sense of intrigue and suspense.

With a passion for the world of art and a fascination with the hidden secrets of history, the author's writing is deeply influenced by a love for both the creative and investigative aspects of storytelling. He has an uncanny ability to draw readers into the world they create, inviting them to become part of the detective's journey, to immerse themselves in the art world's complexities, and to uncover the enigmas that lie beneath the surface.

The author's dedication to research and attention to detail are evident in the way he seamlessly blends historical facts, art-related knowledge, and detective work into his narratives. His commitment to authenticity and accuracy ensures that readers are not only entertained but also enlightened by the wealth of information interwoven into the story.

While the author's identity remains shrouded in mystery, his works have left an indelible mark on the world of mystery and thriller literature. His ability to create compelling narratives, rich with suspense and riddled with secrets, continues to captivate readers, and keep them eagerly turning the pages, yearning to uncover the truth within the enigma. The author's books are a testament to his passion for storytelling and his relentless pursuit of engaging the imagination of his readers.